EXTREME
Space
Tourist
A Traveler's Guide
to the Solar System

Stuart Atkinson

Capstone
press
Mankato, Minnesota

Fact Finders is published by Capstone Press,
a Capstone Publishers company.
151 Good Counsel Drive, P.O. Box 669,
Mankato, Minnesota 56002.
www.capstonepress.com

Produced for A & C Black by

Monkey Puzzle Media Ltd
The Rectory, Eyke, Woodbridge
Suffolk IP12 2QW, UK

Library of Congress Cataloging-in-Publication Data

Atkinson, Stuart.
    Space tourist : a traveler's guide to the solar system / by
Stuart Atkinson.
        p. cm. -- (Fact finders. Extreme!)
    Includes bibliographical references and index.
    Summary: "Presents the science of space exploration
including planet information, space probes, and the
future of space travel"--Provided by publisher.
    ISBN-13: 978-1-4296-3127-3 (hardcover)
    ISBN-10: 1-4296-3127-9 (hardcover)
    ISBN-13: 978-1-4296-3147-1 (softcover)
    ISBN-10: 1-4296-3147-3 (softcover)
1. Manned space flight--Juvenile literature. 2. Solar
system--Juvenile literature. 3. Interplanetary voyages--
Juvenile literature. 4. Space tourism--Juvenile literature.
I. Title. II. Series.

TL793.A8849 2009
629.4--dc22

2008023562

Editor: Steve Parker
Design: Mayer Media Ltd
Picture research: Lynda Lines
Series consultant: Jane Turner

This book is produced using paper that is made from
wood grown in managed, sustainable forests. It is natural,
renewable, and recyclable. The logging and manufacturing
processes conform to the environmental regulations of
the country of origin.

Printed in the United States of America

Picture acknowledgements
Corbis p. 25 bottom (Bettmann); Getty Images pp. 14 top
and 15 top (NASA-JPL-Caltech/Science Faction), 28 (AFP);
MPM Images pp. 7 (Digital Vision), 13 (Digital Vision);
NASA pp. 6–7, 8, 9, 11, 12, 14 bottom, 15 bottom (Pat
Rawlings), 19, 21, 23, 24–25, 25 top, 27; PA Photos p. 16
(AP); Rex Features p. 5; Science Photo Library pp. 1 (Chris
Butler), 4 (Victor Habbick Visions), 10 (Christian Darkin),
17 (Roger Harris), 18 (Detlev van Ravenswaay), 20 (Chris
Butler), 22–23 (David A. Hardy, Futures: 50 Years in
Space), 26 (Robert McNaught), 29 (Victor Habbick
Visions).

The front cover shows an artist's impression of astronauts
on the surface of Mars (Getty Images/ James Porto).

Every effort has been made to contact copyright holders
of material reproduced in this book. Any omissions will be
rectified in subsequent printings if notice is given to the
publishers.

CONTENTS

Abbreviations **m** stands for meters • **ft** stands for feet • **in** stands for inches • **cm** stands for centimeters • **km** stands for kilometers

Leaving Earth

Where have you been on vacation? Perhaps a different town, another country, or even across a continent? Tourists of the future might go still farther. Imagine going on a sightseeing tour of the solar system!

The solar system is the Sun and everything that goes around it. It has eight large **planets**, including our Earth, plus hundreds of smaller **moons** and thousands of other objects. So there'd be lots of exciting sights to see.

If you went on a space vacation, where could you go, and what could you do? Let's find out!

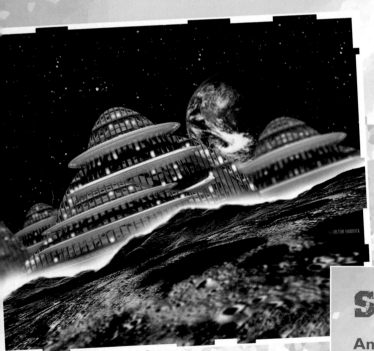

Imagine spending part of your tour in a space hotel like the one in this artist's impression. But you'd need a spacesuit to go outside!

Space-Speak

An object traveling around another object in space is said to **orbit** it. Earth orbits the Sun. If you flew up into space, you would orbit the Earth.

planet a solar system object that's roughly round and is the largest in its area of space

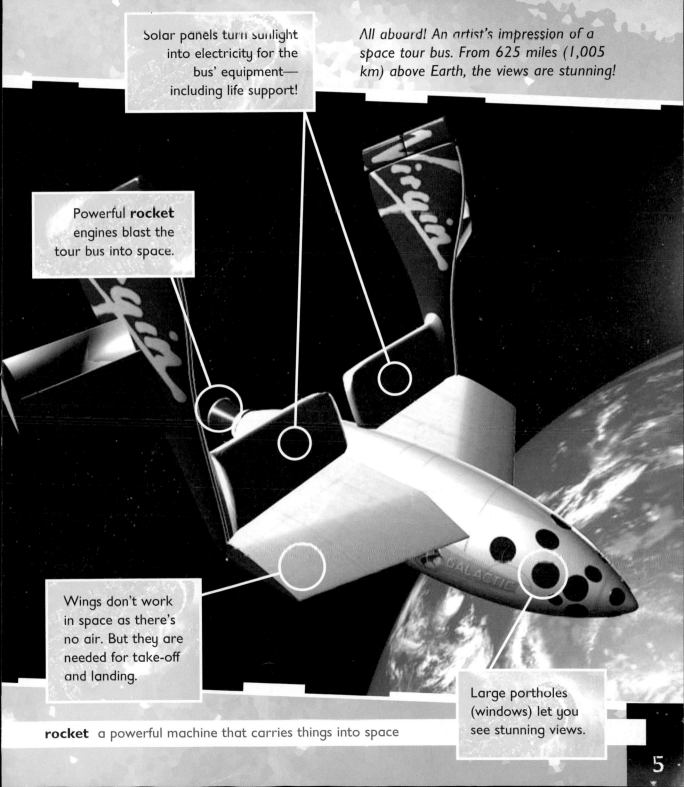

Solar panels turn sunlight into electricity for the bus' equipment—including life support!

All aboard! An artist's impression of a space tour bus. From 625 miles (1,005 km) above Earth, the views are stunning!

Powerful **rocket** engines blast the tour bus into space.

Wings don't work in space as there's no air. But they are needed for take-off and landing.

Large portholes (windows) let you see stunning views.

rocket a powerful machine that carries things into space

5

On the Moon

The Moon is the first stop on your tour. It's only a three-day space flight away from Earth.

When astronauts first landed on the Moon in 1969, they found ash-gray dust, shattered **boulders**, and bowl-shaped craters. Standing on the Moon, you'd see hills and gray plains all around, with Earth shining above like a blue-and-white marble. Because there is no air to make the Moon's sky blue, it's as black as coal. Also the Moon's gravity is weaker than Earth's. So you'd bounce instead of walk, and leap around like a kangaroo!

Imagine stepping off your tour bus here! The Moon has no air or water. Without a spacesuit, you'd be dead in seconds!

Low mountains in the background.

Much of the surface is covered in gray dust.

This low hill formed billions of years ago when the Moon had **volcanoes**.

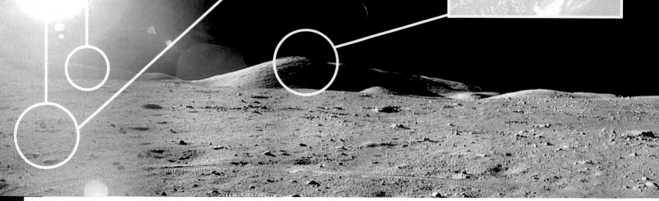

boulders very large pieces of rock or stone

The second person on the Moon was Buzz Aldrin. Because there's no **atmosphere** or weather there, his boot prints in the dust will last for millions of years.

Space-Speak

The Moon orbits the Earth every 28 days. The sunlit part we see from Earth appears to change shape, from new Moon to full Moon.

The **lunar** rover, an electric buggy, is still there on the Moon's surface.

Astronaut Eugene Cernan gathers some Moon rocks to take back home.

atmosphere layers of gas surrounding a space object like a planet or moon

Sun at the center

After the Moon, your exciting tour of the solar system would head for its center—the Sun.

Sunspots are always changing. They grow over a few weeks, then fade away as new ones appear elsewhere. Even a small sunspot is bigger than the whole Earth.

The Sun is a **star**, like all the other stars that twinkle in the night sky. But because it's the closest star to Earth—only 92 million miles (148 million kilometers) away—it looks like a huge ball of fire. (Never look at the Sun through binoculars or a **telescope**, or even without them. You could go blind!) The Sun is so bright because it's incredibly hot. Its surface temperature is 10,800 degrees Fahrenheit (5,982 degrees Celsius), over 30 times hotter than a home oven.

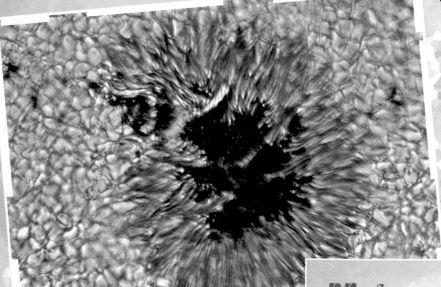

star huge ball of flaming gases in space

Make sure you take pictures of ...

... Sunspots. These are enormous magnetic storms dotted about on the surface of the Sun.

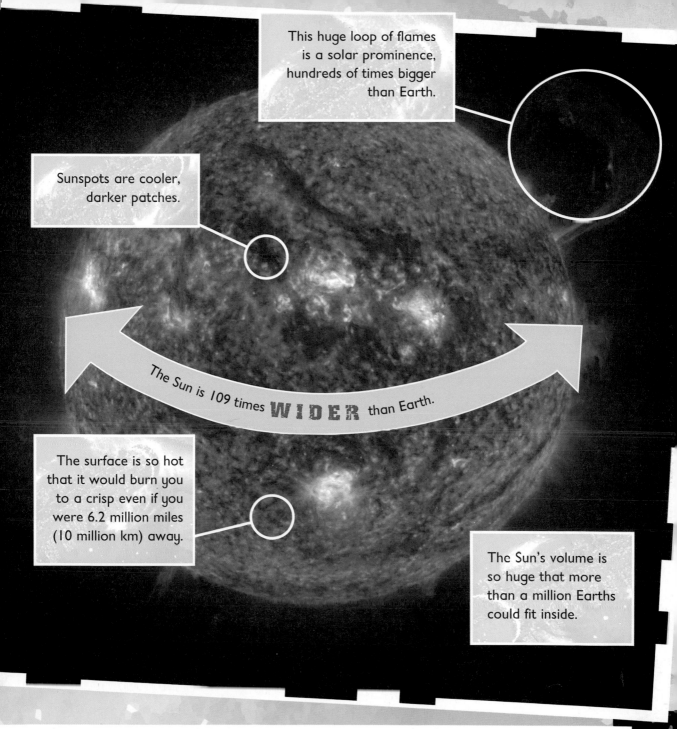

This huge loop of flames is a solar prominence, hundreds of times bigger than Earth.

Sunspots are cooler, darker patches.

The Sun is 109 times **WIDER** than Earth.

The surface is so hot that it would burn you to a crisp even if you were 6.2 million miles (10 million km) away.

The Sun's volume is so huge that more than a million Earths could fit inside.

telescope makes faraway things look nearer

Mercury's furnace

Tiny Mercury is the closest planet to the Sun. It whizzes around the Sun once every 88 Earth days, which is one Mercury year. If you lived there, you'd have a birthday every 88 days!

*Mercury's surface is covered with huge bowl-like craters, cliffs, and **canyons**. The gigantic Caloris Basin crater formed when a piece of space rock 95 miles (153 km) wide hit the planet.*

Because Mercury is so close to the Sun, it's like a furnace. On the surface, it's ten times hotter than in an oven. Yet there may be ice in deep craters near Mercury's poles, at the planet's top and bottom, where the Sun's rays cannot reach.

day time taken for an object, like a planet, to rotate once

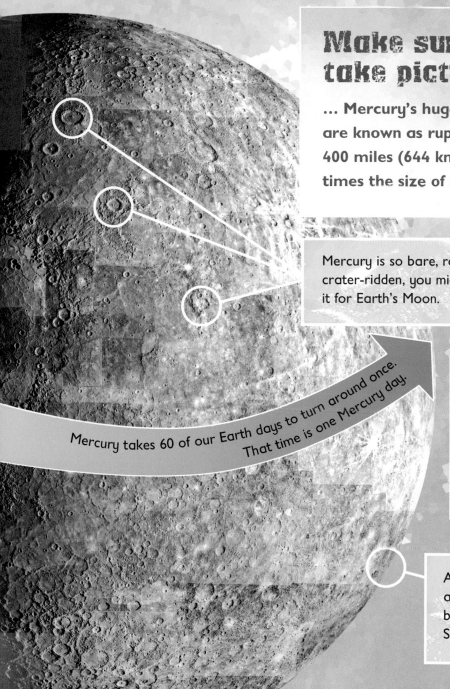

Make sure you take pictures of ...

... Mercury's huge steep cliffs, which are known as rupes. Discovery Rupes is 400 miles (644 km) long, one and a half times the size of Earth's Grand Canyon.

Mercury is so bare, rocky, and crater-ridden, you might mistake it for Earth's Moon.

Mercury takes 60 of our Earth days to turn around once. That time is one Mercury day.

Since a Mercury day is 60 Earth days, and a Mercury year is 88 Earth days, this planet's day is almost three-quarters as long as its year!

Almost all of Mercury's atmosphere has been blasted away by the Sun's incredible heat.

year time taken for an object to travel once around the Sun

Shining Venus

Venus is often visible in the night sky from Earth. When it shines brightly after sunset, it's known as the Evening Star.

Space probes use special radar equipment to see through Venus' clouds to the surface mountains and valleys. The peak on the right is Gula Mons, one-third as high as Earth's Mount Everest

The next planet out from the Sun after Mercury is Venus. It's named after the Roman goddess of love because it shines so beautifully when seen from Earth. This is because its clouds reflect the Sun's rays like a mirror. Many surface features of Venus are also named after famous women from legend and history, such as King Arthur's queen Guinevere and Greek goddess Aphrodite. But when you reach Venus, you'd find it's far from beautiful. It's an ugly, deadly place!

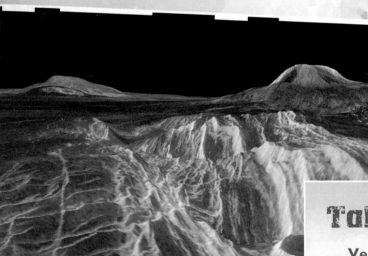

Take pictures of ...

... Venera 7, the first space probe to land on Venus in 1970. Or what's left of it— the acid fumes of Venus's atmosphere may have eaten it all away!

space probe an unmanned spacecraft sent to study objects out in space

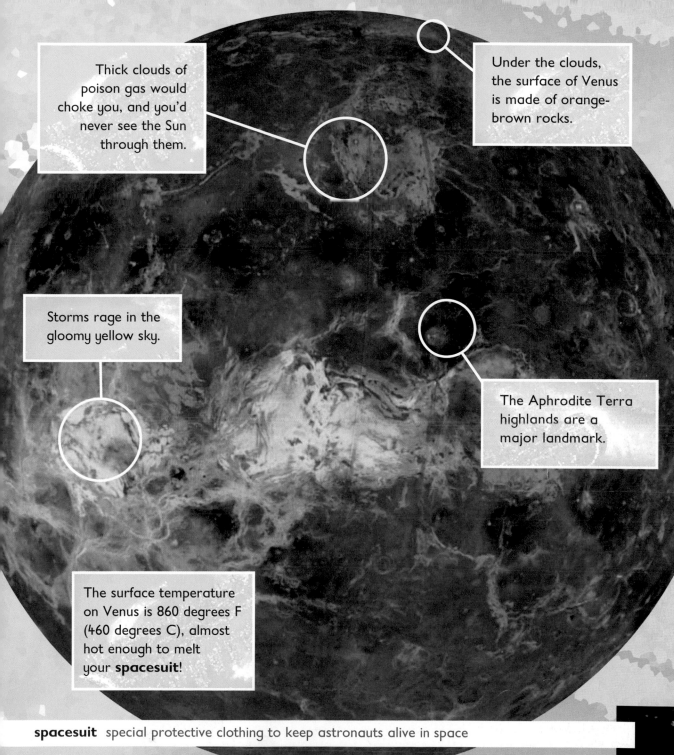

Thick clouds of poison gas would choke you, and you'd never see the Sun through them.

Under the clouds, the surface of Venus is made of orange-brown rocks.

Storms rage in the gloomy yellow sky.

The Aphrodite Terra highlands are a major landmark.

The surface temperature on Venus is 860 degrees F (460 degrees C), almost hot enough to melt your **spacesuit**!

spacesuit special protective clothing to keep astronauts alive in space

Mars, Red Planet

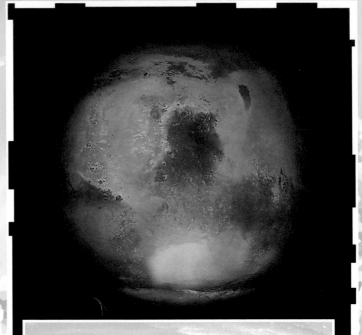

Mars is nicknamed the Red Planet because it looks bright red when seen from Earth. When you arrive, you'd see that its rocky surface really is reddish-brown—because it's made of rust!

The rocks and dust on Mars contain lots of iron oxide, the same substance that's in rust. Mars is only half Earth's size, but it has some gigantic craters, canyons, and mountains. Olympus Mons is three times higher than Mount Everest. If Mariner Valley was on Earth, it would stretch across the United States!

Deadly!

The Martian atmosphere contains poisonous carbon dioxide and methane gases.

Long ago Mars had rivers, lakes, and possibly oceans, but now it's very dry. This is the edge of the 2,500-ft (762-m) wide Victoria Crater.

Mars changes with the seasons. The pictures opposite and below show the two sides of the planet in late summer, with a pale ice cap at the South Pole (bottom). In winter the ice caps at both poles grow.

Mars is farther from the Sun than Earth, and so it's very cold, down to -266 degrees Fahrenheit (-166 degrees Celsius). Whirling winds and dust storms swirl across the plains. Many scientists believe simple forms of life could live under the surface. Have a look if you go!

Massive!

Olympus Mons, an old **volcano**, is the largest mountain in the whole solar system.

Gigantic!

Mariner Valley is like Earth's Grand Canyon, but three times deeper and ten times longer!

Make sure you take pictures of ...

... the Vikings on Mars. But they're not warriors from Norway: they're space probes that landed in 1976.

Hi, everyone at home! Astronauts may get to Mars by 2037.

volcano an opening in a planet's crust through which gases, dust, and other substances erupt

Asteroids everywhere

After Mars, the next stop on your tour is the asteroid belt. Here you'll see thousands of rocky lumps called asteroids.

The Japanese space probe Hayabusa photographed large boulders on the asteroid Itokawa.

Asteroids are leftovers from when the solar system formed, nearly five billion years ago. They orbit the Sun like miniature planets and are basically pieces of a world that never formed. Flying past one, you'd see a huge chunk of stone, or metal, or a mixture of both.

Astronomers keep a close watch for any asteroids passing close to Earth. If one hit us, we could become as extinct as the dinosaurs.

astronomers people who study space and the universe

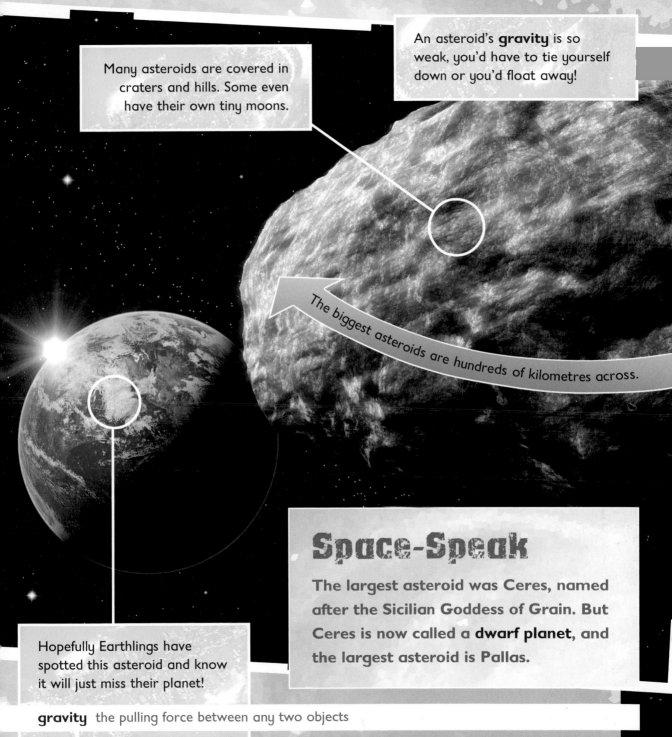

Many asteroids are covered in craters and hills. Some even have their own tiny moons.

An asteroid's **gravity** is so weak, you'd have to tie yourself down or you'd float away!

The biggest asteroids are hundreds of kilometres across.

Space-Speak

The largest asteroid was Ceres, named after the Sicilian Goddess of Grain. But Ceres is now called a **dwarf planet**, and the largest asteroid is Pallas.

Hopefully Earthlings have spotted this asteroid and know it will just miss their planet!

gravity the pulling force between any two objects

Jupiter, King of Planets

You couldn't land on Jupiter because it has no hard, firm surface to land on!

Jupiter is the biggest planet, a **gas giant** made of gases and liquids. From Earth it looks like a bright yellow-blue star, but from your spaceship window, you'd see a huge globe with bands of brown and orange clouds.

Jupiter has more than 60 moons. It also has rings of dust, but these are so dark, they'd be hard to see from your spaceship.

*Jupiter looms huge over the horizon, in this view from its moon Io. Volcanoes on Io pour out gas and fumes. Some astronomers think there might be **alien** life beneath the frozen surface of another Jupiter moon, Europa.*

alien not from or to do with Earth

Violent!

White and yellow storms whirl around Jupiter and tear each other into tiny pieces if they come too close.

Crusher!

Jupiter's center is a rocky core as big as Earth. No spaceship could ever get there—the pressure would squash it like a rotten tomato.

The light bands are Jupiter's highest clouds, with dark bands of lower clouds between.

The clouds stretch out into long bands because Jupiter whirls around so fast—once every 10 hours.

The Great Red Spot is an enormous hurricane twice the size of Earth.

Rings of Saturn

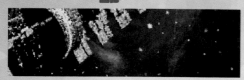

Saturn is a gas giant planet, like Jupiter. It's most famous for its fantastic, beautiful rings.

We now know that Jupiter and other planets have rings. But Saturn is still known as the Ringed Planet, because its rings are biggest and brightest. They look solid from a distance, like hoops. As you fly through them, you'd see they're actually made of billions of chunks of ice! Saturn has over 60 moons. Tiny Mimas is nicknamed the Death Star Moon because it looks like the evil battle station in the *Star Wars* films.

On a very clear day, this could be your view of Saturn from its largest moon, Titan. This massive moon is bigger than planet Mercury. Titan has lakes and seas of poisonous chemicals!

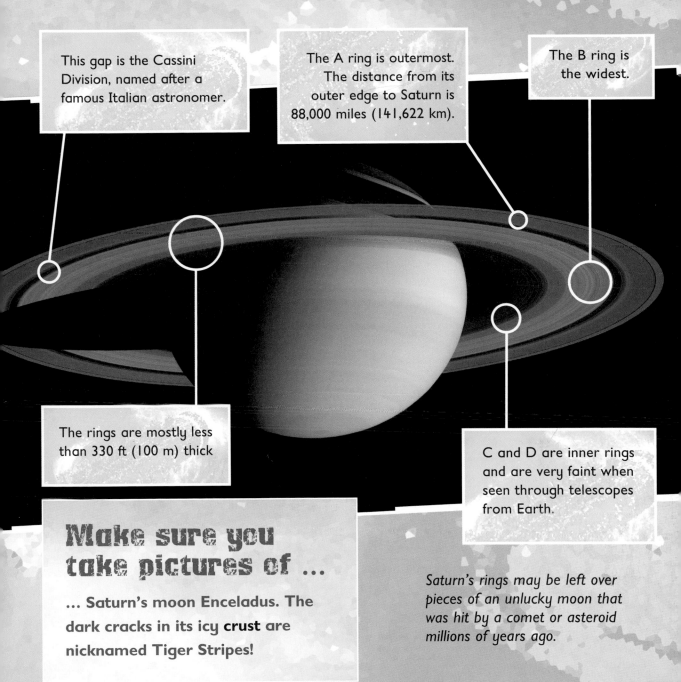

This gap is the Cassini Division, named after a famous Italian astronomer.

The A ring is outermost. The distance from its outer edge to Saturn is 88,000 miles (141,622 km).

The B ring is the widest.

The rings are mostly less than 330 ft (100 m) thick

C and D are inner rings and are very faint when seen through telescopes from Earth.

Make sure you take pictures of ...

... Saturn's moon Enceladus. The dark cracks in its icy **crust** are nicknamed Tiger Stripes!

Saturn's rings may be left over pieces of an unlucky moon that was hit by a comet or asteroid millions of years ago.

crust the hard outer surface of a planet or object

Uranus and Neptune

As you approach Uranus and Neptune, sit back and enjoy the view. These planets have amazing delicate colors, due to the gases swirling around in their atmospheres.

Space-Speak

The Great Dark Spot is Neptune's famous storm—or was. Discovered in 1989, it had strangely vanished by 1994.

Triton's mini-volcanoes, called **geysers**, blow out gases and mysterious dark material.

If you visit Neptune's moon Triton, watch out. You could be blown away by a volcano!

Cliffs and plunging valleys make Triton travel tricky.

Uranus and Neptune are gas giant planets, but smaller than Jupiter and Saturn. Uranus looks pale milky-green, while Neptune appears more turquoise-blue.

Uranus is strange because it's tipped over on its side and rolls around the Sun like a barrel, whereas the other planets spin upright, like tops. Astronomers think Uranus was knocked off balance when something hit it billions of years ago. Neptune is the farthest planet from the Sun, at 30 times more distant than Earth.

Uranus is weird. It has four main rings and more than 25 moons, and it spins on its side!

Neptune shines with an eerie glow in Triton's black, star-studded sky.

Neptune's winds are the fastest in the solar system, at 1,250 mph (2,012 km/h)!

geysers springs that shoot out jets of substances

Pluto at the edge

At last you've reached the farthest point of your tour. Pluto is so distant in the solar system that the Sun just looks like any other bright star.

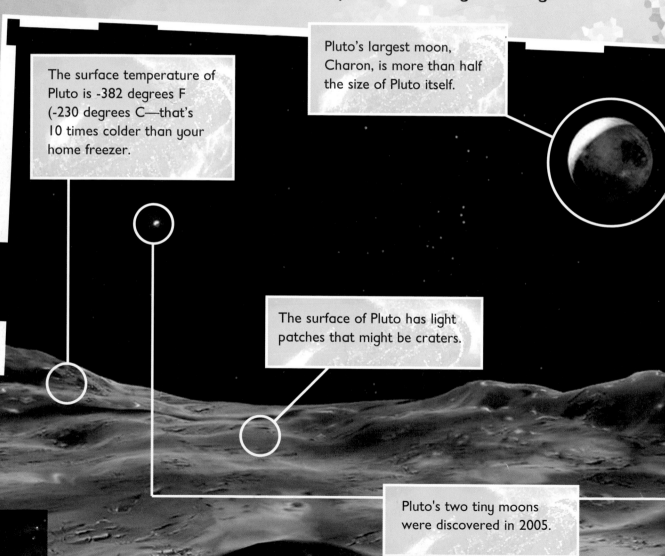

Pluto's largest moon, Charon, is more than half the size of Pluto itself.

The surface temperature of Pluto is -382 degrees F (-230 degrees C—that's 10 times colder than your home freezer.

The surface of Pluto has light patches that might be craters.

Pluto's two tiny moons were discovered in 2005.

Pluto is small, cold, and has a strange oval, lopsided orbit. Even farther away from the Sun than Pluto are Kuiper Belt Objects, KBOs. They are probably similar to Pluto, and some take even longer to orbit the Sun. One called Sedna takes over 10,000 Earth years for one orbit!

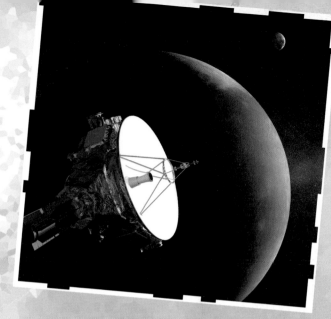

New Horizons will take eight years to reach Pluto. Hopefully your tour bus would be much quicker!

Pluto timeline

1930 Pluto is discovered by Clyde Tombaugh.

1992 Astronomers find other large objects past Pluto, called **KBOs**.

2005 Eris is discovered, a **KBO** bigger than Pluto.

2006 Astronomers decide Pluto is not a full planet but a dwarf planet.

2015 New Horizons probe will fly past Pluto and take close-up pictures. What will they show?

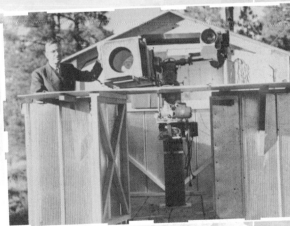

Pluto's discoverer, Clyde Tombaugh.

Comet encounter

During your trip, you might be lucky enough to see a comet, with its bright head and long glowing tail, or maybe two tails!

Once people believed that comets brought disasters such as earthquakes, floods, and even the death of kings. Now we know they are giant dusty icebergs, whose orbits take them far from the Sun. If your tour bus could fly alongside a comet, you would see it start to melt as it neared the Sun. Bits of dust and gas come away to form long, glowing tails.

A comet's bright head contains the icy nucleus. The feathery tails do not trail behind but always point away from the Sun.

Space-Speak

The icy center of a comet's head, called its nucleus, can be more than 30 miles (48 km) across.

Dateline 2005
Spacecraft Deep Impact approaches the icy nucleus of Comet Tempel 2.

Gush!
Gas and dust shoot out from the impact site.

Whoosh!
The craft fires a probe into the nucleus.

Wham!
The probe slams into the nucleus.

Snap!
Deep Impact photographs the event and sends the pictures by radio back to Earth.

27

Will it ever happen?

Could people ever go on a real space vacation around the solar system? Not for at least a hundred years.

In just a few years, people will be flying into space on short sightseeing trips. Right now, many companies are designing small spaceships to carry a few people into space. There are even plans for small hotels where tourists could enjoy a week's stay in orbit. Maybe you will, too!

You would train for your trip at a space center, to learn about **zero gravity** and dreaded space sickness! You might take off from a spaceport, like an airport for spaceships. Make sure you get a window seat, for amazing views of Earth's oceans, clouds, and countries. But even a two-hour space trip will cost a small fortune!

Training for zero gravity can be fun—or make you throw up!

Space-Speak

Space tourists will train in a special airplane that simulates zero gravity. It can make you feel sick, so it's called the Vomit Comet!

zero gravity no gravity, so things are weightless

A solar system round trip might take many years.
The tour bus would need a massive cargo spaceship
like this to bring food, water, fuel, and other needs.

Glossary

alien not from or to do with Earth

asteroid a solar system object smaller than a planet that orbits the Sun

astronomers people who study space and the universe

atmosphere layers of gas surrounding a space object like a planet or moon

boulders very large pieces of rock or stone

canyon a deep narrow valley with steep sides

crust the hard outer surface of a planet or object

day time taken for an object like a planet to rotate once

dwarf planet a solar system body smaller than a planet but larger than an asteroid

gas giant a huge planet made mostly of gas and liquid

geysers springs that shoot out jets of substances

gravity the pulling force between any two objects

lunar relating to the Moon

moon a smaller object that goes around a larger one, usually a planet

orbit to go or revolve around another object in space

planet a solar system object that's roughly round and is the largest in its area of space

rocket a powerful machine that carries things into space

solar system the Sun and all the planets, moons, asteroids, and other objects that revolve around it

space probe an unmanned spacecraft sent to study objects out in space

spacesuit special protective clothing to keep astronauts alive in space

star huge ball of flaming gases in space

telescope instrument that makes faraway things look nearer

volcano an opening in a planet's crust through which gases, dust and other substances erupt

year time taken for an object to travel once around the Sun

zero gravity no gravity, so things are weightless, as in space

Further information

Activities

- If there's an observatory where you live, ask to go there and talk to the astronomers about the solar system and maybe look through the telescope.

- Check if your local museum or exhibition center has any exhibits or talks about space.

- Find out if your town has an astronomical society. You can go to their meetings to learn a lot more about planets and space exploration.

Web sites

FactHound offers a safe, fun way to find Internet sites related to this book. All of the sites on FactHound have been researched by our staff. Visit *www.facthound.com* for age-appropriate sites. You may browse subjects by clicking on letters, or by clicking on pictures and words.
FactHound will fetch the best sites for you!

Films

Blue Planet directed by Ben Burtt (IMAX, 1993) Amazing images of the Earth from space as seen by space shuttle astronauts.

The Dream Is Alive directed by Graeme Ferguson (IMAX, 1985) How astronauts live and work in space.

Apollo 13 directed by Ron Howard (MCA/ Universal Pictures, 1995) One of the best space movies, telling the amazing true story of the unlucky Apollo 13 Moon mission.

Index